GUIDELINES FOR THE
OF GENERAL DAMAGES
IN PERSONAL INJURY CASES

GUIDELINES FOR THE ASSESSMENT OF GENERAL DAMAGES IN PERSONAL INJURY CASES

Third Edition

Compiled for the

Judicial Studies Board

by

**John Cherry, QC; Edwin Glasgow, QC;
D. A. K. Hughes, Solicitor; R. J. Sutcliffe, Solicitor;
His Honour Judge Roger Cox**

Foreword by The Right Hon. Lord Woolf
Master of the Rolls

BLACKSTONE
PRESS LIMITED

First published in Great Britain 1992 by Blackstone Press Limited,
9-15 Aldine Street, London W12 8AW. Telephone 0181-740 2277

© Judicial Studies Board, 1992

First edition 1992
Reprinted 1992
Reprinted 1993
Reprinted 1994
Second edition 1994
Reprinted 1994
Reprinted 1996
Third edition 1996

ISBN: 1 85431 577 3

British Library Cataloguing in Publication Data
A CIP catalogue record for this book is available from the British Library.

Typeset by Style Photosetting Limited, Mayfield, East Sussex
Printed by Ashford Colour Press, Gosport, Hampshire

Contents

Foreword by Lord Woolf MR

My two predecessors as Master of the Rolls warmly praised the authors of this excellent book. I echo their praise. To this I add congratulations on their timing. To produce three editions of this book in four and a half years and to receive the endorsement of a different Master of the Rolls for each edition over that short period of time is sufficiently remarkable to cause me some concern, as to the date on which the next edition will appear in relation to my future!

That a new edition will appear, I have no doubt. This book has been a runaway success because it meets a real demand on the part of the judiciary, the profession and everyone else involved in personal injury litigation.

Having recently completed my report on Access to Justice, I am particularly conscious of the value of this book. It can, in the case of personal injury litigation, assist in fulfilling the objectives which the report wishes to achieve. One of my aims is that whenever possible litigation is avoided. Here when the real issue is quantum, the use of this book should place both sides in approximately the same area in the scale of damages. This should facilitate settlements. It will provide a broad tariff within which the parties should find it relatively easy to compromise their differences. Where litigation is necessary, then it will help both the claimant and the defendant to take advantage of the proposed procedural changes and make realistic offers to settle. These will play a central part in the new approach to litigation. It will also assist in achieving greater consistency and certainty in the decisions of judges when offers to settle are rejected. It will help judges to determine whether the attitude to damages which the parties are adopting is reasonable. This will be important in determining issues as to costs.

This book, of course is not in itself exhaustive on the subject of quantum in the areas with which it deals. Usually it will be the starting off point rather than the last word on the appropriate award in any particular case. This has been fully explained by my two predecessors but it does not detract from the contribution which this book can make. Especially in the case of appellate judges, it is important that they are kept up to date as to the value of the most common categories of injuries. It is so easy for an appellate judge to lose touch with the current tariff unless there is a book of this sort which can provide a reliable check against which the decision in a particular case can be evaluated. Previous decisions of the Court of Appeal can be unreliable guides as to the generality of cases because they are often influenced by the decision in the Court below.

As Lord Bingham said in his Foreword 'a consensus is as desirable in principle if different claimants are to be treated fairly, one as compared with another'. I therefore very much hope that judges of first instance and appellate judges will continue to use this book in the manner described by Lord Donaldson and Lord Bingham in the previous Forewords.

I am aware of the dicta of one member of the Court of Appeal in the case of *Arafa* v *Potter* [1994] PIQRQ 73 at p. 79. If the dicta was intended to suggest that the Court of Appeal should not regard this book as a source from which an approximate figure for damages can be obtained, I profoundly disagree. The other member of the Court in fact referred to this book in the course of his judgment as a check as to what the correct bracket of damages should be. He was entitled to do so. Unless Court of Appeal judges as well as judges at first instance have regard to the guidelines contained in this book, its purpose will be defeated. As in the past so in the future it should be used not only because it is convenient to do so, but because due to the way in which it is compiled and because of its extensive use, it is the most reliable tool, which up to now has been made available to courts up and down the land as to what is the correct range of damages for common classes of injuries.

Lord Woolf
Master of the Rolls
Royal Courts of Justice
18 October 1996

Foreword to the Second Edition by Sir Thomas Bingham MR

How can a precisely calculated arithmetical price tag be put on a personal injury such as the loss of a leg, or impairment of hearing, or psychiatric damage? That is a question often and reasonably asked by lawyer and non-lawyer alike. There are two answers.

The first is that it cannot. Personal injuries cannot, like damage to chattels, be valued by reference to the cost of repair or the reduction in the market value of the damaged article. But the law recognises that claimants who have suffered personal injury should be compensated, and money is the only available medium of compensation. That leads on to the second answer, which is that while mathematical precision is unattainable some broad working consensus on the appropriate level of compensation for different injuries is highly desirable both in principle and in practice.

Such a consensus is desirable in principle if different claimants are to be treated fairly, one as compared with another. The level of award should not depend on the arbitrary whim of the judge. It is desirable in practice because without it a claimant (and his advisers) will not know what to accept nor a defendant (and his advisers) what to offer. Nor will the judge know what, in fairness to the claimant who will receive and the defendant who will pay, he should award.

This book, summarising the experience and research of an expert working party established by the Judicial Studies Board, seeks to record the broad effect of the current consensus in relation to different classes of injury. It does not seek to force all cases into an ill-fitting straitjacket. It does not ignore the obvious fact that no two cases, even if they involve the same injury, are the same. It recognises that injuries vary in severity and may affect different claimants in differing ways and to differing degrees. It does not seek to deprive the judge of the power to decide, after all the evidence has been heard, what is the right sum to award in a given case. But it does mark out the target area. It does indicate the range of awards likely to be made, on the basis of past awards and current practice, in the ordinary run of case.

The first edition of this book was published in 1992. It proved a runaway success, an invaluable aid to judges and practitioners alike. So much so that a new edition is already needed, to take account of recent trends and awards. The same careful, methodical work has gone into this edition as into its predecessor. There can be no doubt that it will enjoy the same success. Everyone conerned in any capacity in the difficult and important task of assessing damages for personal injury will wish it well.

The Right Hon. Sir Thomas Bingham
Master of the Rolls
Royal Courts of Justice
25 July 1994

Foreword to the First Edition
by Lord Donaldson of Lymington

Paradoxical as it may seem, one of the commonest tasks of a judge sitting in a civil court is also one of the most difficult. This is the assessment of general damages for pain, suffering or loss of the amenities of life. Since no monetary award can compensate in any real sense, these damages cannot be assessed by a process of calculation. Yet whilst no two cases are ever precisely the same, justice requires that there be consistency between awards.

The solution to this dilemma has lain in using the amount of damages awarded in reported cases as guidelines or markers and seeking to slot the particular case into the framework thus provided. This is easier stated than done, because reports of the framework cases are scattered over a variety of publications and not all the awards appear, from the sometimes brief reports, to be consistent with one another. Furthermore some of the older cases are positively misleading unless account is taken of changes in the value of money and the process of revaluation is far from being an exact science.

It was against this background that the Judicial Studies Board set up a working party under the chairmanship of Judge Roger Cox to prepare 'Guidelines for Assessment of General Damages in Personal Injury Cases'. It was not intended to represent, and does not represent, a new or different approach to the problem. Nor is it intended to be a 'ready reckoner' or in any way to fetter the individual judgment which must be brought to bear upon the unique features of each particular case. What it is intended to do, and what it does quite admirably, is to distil the conventional wisdom contained in the reported cases, to supplement it from the collective experience of the working party and to present the result in a convenient, logical and coherent form.

There can be no doubt about the practical value of this report and it has been agreed by the four Heads of Division that it shall be circulated to all judges, recorders and district judges who may be concerned with the assessment of general damages in personal injury cases. We also consider that it should be made available to the two branches of the practising profession and to any others who would be assisted by it.

Judges and practitioners will, as always, remain free to take full account of the amount of damages awarded in earlier cases, but it is hoped that with the publication of this report this will less often be necessary. They will also need to take account of cases reported after the effective date of the working party's report since that report, while to some extent providing a new baseline is not intended to, and could not, freeze the scale of damages either absolutely or in relative terms as between different categories of loss.

May I convey my sincere congratulations to the authors upon the excellent way in which they have performed their task.

Lord Donaldson of Lymington
25 March 1992

Introduction

In reconsidering these guidelines for a third edition of this book, the working party set up by the Civil and Family Committee of the Judicial Studies Board in 1990 has once more returned to the source material. It has not confined itself to consideration of reported cases, but has, as it did for previous editions, considered many decisions and settlements which have been drawn to the attention of its members by judges and professional colleagues. It seems that those who are responsible for the reporting of cases in law reports and journals have tended, for quite understandable reasons, to concentrate on the exceptional cases, so that reference only to those sources may produce a somewhat distorted picture.

The whole object of this book is to give guidance to judges, practitioners and all those concerned in the assessment of damages as to the way in which courts have approached this very difficult topic. The working party is not seeking to fetter the discretion of the tribunal awarding compensation but to assist it to arrive at the appropriate figure. The doctrine of *stare decisis* does not apply in this field and so it cannot in any circumstances be said that this book presents the law on the subject. Nevertheless it is hoped that reference to these guidelines will be of help when it becomes necessary to consider individual reported awards which are of course related to individual plaintiffs. At the same time and for the same reasons the text of this volume should not be construed with the same minuteness as that of a statute.

In some of the areas covered in this book the main concern has been with changes in the value of money since the last edition was prepared. In the assessment of damages, taking account of inflation is not an exact science. The assessor will not want to produce an award exact to the last decimal place, but rather to award a round figure which represents fair compensation for the injury sustained. Hence it is important to examine the trend of awards to see if they are keeping up with inflation or falling behind or outstripping it.

A particular trend which seems to have emerged in the last few years has caused the working party some concern. It is the extent to which in recent cases emphasis on the subjective reaction of a Plaintiff to the physical injuries and the circumstances in which they were sustained has been used as a means of inflating the award of damages. Every injured person suffers a reaction to the situation and its causes and that reaction has always been considered in the assessment of damages for pain and *suffering*. A clear example of this approach is to be found in the chapter of this book dealing with facial injuries. Such an approach must be separated carefully from the wholly distinct head of damage which is post-traumatic stress disorder, the definition of which is set out in general terms in chapter 3. Unless that condition exists, it is suggested that the general guidelines are appropriate.

The working party is once more immensely grateful to the very large number of judges, practitioners and others working in the field of personal injury litigation who have taken the trouble to offer comment, criticism and encouragement. None of the advice thus tendered has been ignored but not all of it has been incorporated in this edition. The working party is genuinely interested in opinions about areas where damages are perceived to be too low or too high but the purpose of this guide is not to preach but rather to reflect the approach adopted by those who assess damages. There are areas where members of the working party feel quite strongly that the awards indicated by the decisions are inappropriate but they have resisted the temptation to express their own opinions in this book, even where all are agreed. At the same time no member of the working party feels inhibited in his professional role from arguing for or awarding in a proper case damages which do not appear to fall within the guidelines.

Particular thanks are due to the Judicial Studies Board and to its publications coordinator, Jaqueline Lefton. Without their help this new edition would not have been possible.

The figures put forward in this edition take account of cases of which the members of the working party have become aware up to September 1996.

1. Injuries involving Paralysis

(a) Quadriplegia   £110,000 to £130,000

Considerations affecting the level of the award:

(i)   Extent of residual movement

(ii)   Pain

(iii) Effect on other senses

(iv)   Depression

(v)   Age and life expectancy

(b) Paraplegia   £85,000 to £100,000

Considerations affecting the level of the award:

(i)   Pain

(ii)   Depression

(iii) Age and life expectancy

(iv)   The presence or degree of risk of in-
       creasing paralysis resulting, for
       example, from syringomyelia.

3

2. Head Injuries

(a) Very Severe Brain Damage £105,000 to £130,000

In the most severe cases the Plaintiff will be in a vegetative state; there may be recovery of eye opening and some return of sleep and waking rhythm and postural reflex movements; no evidence of meaningful response to environment. Unable to obey commands; no language functions and need for 24-hour nursing care.

Considerations affecting the level of the award:

(i)   Insight

(ii)   Life expectancy

(iii)   Extent of physical limitations

Where the vegetative state is persistent and short lived *and* it is accepted that there is no awareness at all, the award will be solely for loss of amenity and will fall below the above bracket.

(b) Moderately Severe Brain Damage £80,000 to £100,000

Severe disability. Conscious, but total dependency and requiring constant care. Dis-

4

abilities may be physical, e.g. limb paralysis, or cognitive, with marked impairment of intellect and personality. Considerations affecting the level of the award:

(i)   Insight

(ii)   Life expectancy

(iii)   Extent of physical limitations

(c) Moderate Brain Damage

    (i)   Cases in which there is moderate to severe intellectual deficit, a personality change, an effect on sight, speech and senses with a significant risk of epilepsy.   £60,000 to £85,000

    (ii)   Cases in which there is a modest to moderate intellectual deficit, the ability to work is greatly reduced if not removed and there is some risk of epilepsy.   £37,500 to £55,000

    (iii)   Concentration and memory are affected, the ability to work is reduced and there may be a small risk of epilepsy.   £18,500 to £37,500

(d) Minor Brain Damage   £6,000 to £18,500

A good recovery will have been made. The Plaintiff can participate in normal social life and return to work but restoration of all normal functions is not implicit. There may still be persistent defects such as poor concentration and memory or disinhibition of mood which may interfere with lifestyle, leisure activity and future work prospects.

Considerations affecting the level of the award:

(i)   Extent and severity of the initial injury

(ii)   Extent of any continuing and possibly permanent disability

(iii)   Extent of any personality change

(e) Minor Head Injury   £1,000 to £5,500

These are cases where there is *no* evidence of brain damage.

Considerations affecting the level of the award:

(i)   Severity of initial injury

(ii)   Period of recovery from severe symptoms

(iii)   Extent of continuing symptoms at trial

(iv)   Headaches

(f) Established Epilepsy

Grand mal	£42,500 to £60,000
Petit mal	£25,000 to £50,000

The factors which will affect the award will be:

(i)   The existence of other associated behavioural problems.

(ii)   Whether attacks are successfully controlled by medication and the extent to which the appreciation of the quality of life may be blunted by that medication.

6

3. Psychiatric Damage

Some of the figures in the first part of this chapter include an element of post-traumatic stress disorder. It is, of course, not the only psychiatric injury the victim can suffer and a number of the awards on which the figures are based did not reflect this element at all. A separate section dealing with damages where post-traumatic stress disorder is the sole psychiatric illness follows this one.

(A) Psychiatric Damage Generally

The factors to be taken into account in valuing claims for psychiatric damage are as follows:

    (i)   Ability to cope with life and particularly work

    (ii)   Effect on relationships with family etc.

    (iii)   Extent to which treatment would be successful

    (iv)   Future vulnerability

    (v)   Prognosis

    (vi)   The extent and/or nature of any associated physical injuries

    (vii)   Whether medical help has been sought

(a) **Severe Psychiatric Damage**   £25,000 to £50,000

In these cases there will be displayed all of
factors (i) to (vi) above to a marked degree and
the prognosis will invariably be very poor.

(b) **Moderately Severe Psychiatric Damage**   £9,000 to £22,500

Most of factors (i) to (vi) above will be present
to a significant degree but the prognosis will
be generally much more optimistic.

(c) **Moderate Psychiatric Damage**   £2,750 to £8,000

The factors mentioned above will have been
present but there will have been marked
improvement by trial and the prognosis for
those remaining will be good.

(d) **Minor Psychiatric Damage**   £500 to £1,600

This category may include cases where no
medical help has been sought but they will be
rare.

Considerations as to the level of the award will
include the length of the period of disability
and the extent to which daily activities were
affected.

(B) Post-traumatic Stress Disorder

Cases within this category are concerned exclusive-
ly with a specific reactive psychiatric disorder,
according to diagnostic criteria, in which character-
istic symptoms are displayed following a psycho-
logically distressing event outside the range of
normal human experience which would be markedly distressing to almost anyone. Such symptoms
affect basic functions such as breathing, pulse rate
and bowel and/or bladder control. They also
involve persistent re-experiencing of the relevant

event, difficulty in controlling temper, in concentrating and sleeping, and exaggerated startled response.

(a) Severe   £27,000 to £37,500

Such cases will involve permanent effects which prevent the victim from working at all or at least from functioning at anything approaching the pre-trauma level. All aspects of life will be badly affected.

(b) Moderately Severe   £11,000 to £21,500

In such cases the prognosis is for some recovery with professional help but the effects are still likely to cause significant disability for the foreseeable future.

(c) Moderate   £3,250 to £8,000

In these cases the victim is largely recovered and continuing effects are not grossly disabling.

(d) Minor   £1,600 to £3,250

Where a full recovery is made within two to three years or only minor symptoms persist over any longer period.

4. Injuries affecting the Senses

Loss of or damage to senses can be restricted purely to one particular sense, e.g. loss of one eye or total blindness or loss of the sense of smell. However, very often damage to senses can be associated with other injuries. In such cases damages are likely to be viewed as 'multiple injuries' awards.

(A) Injuries affecting Sight

(a) Total Blindness and Deafness £130,000

Such cases must be considered as ranking with the most devastating of injuries.

(b) Total Blindness £97,500

(c) Total Loss of One Eye £24,500 to £27,000

(d) Loss of Sight in One Eye with Reduced Vision in the Remaining Eye

(i) Where there is serious risk of further deterioration in the remaining eye, going beyond the normal risk of sympathetic ophthalmia. £40,000 to £70,000

      (ii)   Where there is reduced vision in the remaining eye and including any problems of, e.g. double vision.   £27,000 to £46,000

(e) Complete Loss of Sight in One Eye   £21,500 to £24,500

This award takes account of the virtually universal risk of sympathetic ophthalmia. The upper end of the bracket is appropriate where there is scarring in the region of the eye, where an artificial eye has been necessary or where there is other cosmetic deformity.

(f) Cases of serious but incomplete loss of vision in one eye without significant risk of loss of or reduction in vision in the remaining eye, or where there is constant double vision.   £10,750 to £17,250

(g) Minor but permanent impairment of vision in one eye including cases where there is some double vision which may not be constant.   £5,500 to £8,750

(h) Minor Eye Injuries   £1,750 to £3,750

In this bracket fall cases of minor but not trivial injuries, such as being struck in the eye, exposure to fumes, smoke or being splashed by liquids, causing initial pain, and some interference with vision, but no lasting effects.

(B) Deafness

The word 'deafness' is used to embrace total and partial hearing loss. In assessing awards for hearing loss regard must be had to the following.

      (i)   Whether the injury is one that has an immediate effect, allowing no opportunity to adapt, or whether it occurred over a period of time, as in noise exposure cases.

    (ii)   Whether the injury or disability is one
that the Plaintiff has suffered at an early
age with the result that it has had or will
have an effect on his speech, or if it is
one that he has suffered in later life.

    (iii)   Whether the injury or disability affects
balance.

(a)   Total Deafness and Loss of Speech   £45,000 to £57,000

Such cases arise, for example, where deafness
has occurred at an early age (e.g. rubella
infection) so as to prevent or seriously affect
speech.

(b)   Total Deafness   £37,500 to £45,000

The lower end of the bracket is appropriate for
cases where there is no speech deficit or
tinnitus. The higher end is appropriate for
cases involving both of these aspects.

(c)   Total Loss of Hearing in One Ear   £14,500 to £20,000

Cases will tend to the higher end of the bracket
where there are associated problems, such as
tinnitus, dizziness or headaches.

(d)   Partial Hearing Loss/Tinnitus

This category covers the bulk of deafness
cases which usually result from exposure to
noise over a prolonged period. The disability
is not to be judged simply by the degree of
hearing loss; there is often a degree of tinnitus
present. The Plaintiff's age is particularly
relevant because impairment of hearing af-
flicts most people in the fullness of time.

    (i)   Severe tinnitus/hearing loss   £13,000 to £20,000

    (ii)   Moderate tinnitus/hearing loss   £6,500 to £13,000

| (iii) | Mild tinnitus with some hearing loss | £6,000 to £6,500 |

| (iv) | Slight or occasional mild tinnitus with slight hearing loss | £3,250 to £5,500 |

(C) Impairment of Taste and Smell

(a) Total Loss of Taste and Smell £17,250

(b) Total Loss of Smell and Significant Loss of Taste £14,500 to £17,250

It must be remembered that in nearly all cases of loss of smell there is some impairment of taste. Such cases fall into the next bracket.

(c) Loss of Smell £11,250 to £14,500

(d) Loss of Taste £8,500 to £11,250

13

5. Injuries to Internal Organs

(A) Chest Injuries

This is a specially difficult area because the vast majority of cases relate to industrial *disease* as distinct from traumatic *injury* and the level of the appropriate award for lung disease necessarily reflects the prognosis for the future and/or the risks of development of secondary sequelae (such as mesothelioma).

Cases of traumatic damage to or loss of a lung are rare: the range is as wide as £1,000 to £50,000.

(a)   The very worst case is of total removal of one lung with considerable and prolonged pain and suffering and permanent serious scarring will be in the region of the maximum award for chest injuries.   £57,000

(b)   Traumatic injury to lungs and heart causing permanent damage, impairment of function, physical disability and reduction of life expectancy is in the region of   £40,000

(c)   Any *injury* affecting lung function and permanent damage to tissue is likely to be in the region of   £5,750 to £8,000

(d)   Smoke inhalation, which often leaves some residual damage not serious enough permanently to interfere with lung function   £2,500 to £5,750

14

(e) Injuries leading to collapsed lungs from which a full and uncomplicated recovery is made   £1,000 to £2,250

(f) Fractures of ribs, which usually cause serious pain and disability over a relatively short time   Up to £1,500

(B) Lung Disease

Reported cases over many years were usually assessed by reference to the Medical Research Council grading system. The brackets set out below have, where appropriate, been cross-referenced to these grades. In many cases a provisional award may be appropriate.

(a) For a young Plaintiff where there is probability of progressive worsening leading to premature death, the award will be up to   £50,000

(b) Severe and worsening impairment of breathing where death within a few years of trial is inevitable or where death follows some years of increasingly painful and disabling symptoms (formerly Grade 5)   £38,000 to £43,000

(c) Cases of severe impairment of lung function with seriously disabling consequences and inevitable loss of life expectancy (formerly Grade 5)   Up to £38,000

(d) Significant impairment of function including cases where pleural plaques are present and where there is a serious risk of the development of asbestosis or mesothelioma (formerly Grade 4)   £20,000 to £22,500

(e) Measurable impairment of function with a real risk of future deterioration (formerly Grade 3), with the cancer risk left for a future award.   £17,000 to £20,000

(f) Benign asbestosis with pleural thickening but no present risk of functional impairment or of cancer is valued in the region of   £5,750

(C) Asthma

(a) Severe and permanent disabling asthma, causing prolonged and regular coughing, sleep disturbed by coughing bouts, significant impairment of physical activity and enjoyment of life and restriction of employment prospects, in the region of   £20,000

(b) Asthma causing some breathing difficulties, the need to use an inhaler from time to time and inability to tolerate smoky environments, with uncertain prognosis, in the region of   £15,000

(c) Some bronchitis and wheezing, not seriously affecting working or social life, with likelihood of substantial recovery within a few years of the exposure to the cause, in the region of   £10,000

(d) Mild asthma, bronchitis, colds and chest problems (usually resulting from unfit housing or similar exposure, particularly in cases of young children) treated by general practitioner and resolving within a few months   £1,000 to £2,000

(D) Digestive System

It is to be noted that the risk of associated damage to the reproductive organs is frequently

16

encountered in cases of this nature and requires separate consideration.

(a) Severe damage with continuing pain or discomfort. £19,000 to £27,000

(b) Serious non-penetrating injury causing long-standing or permanent complications, e.g., severe indigestion, aggravated by physical strain. £7,500 to £12,500

(c) Penetrating stab wounds or industrial laceration or serious seat-belt pressure cases. £2,750 to £5,750

(E) Reproductive System

Male

(a) Total impotence and loss of sexual function in the case of a young man. In the region of £60,000

Cases at the very serious level will frequently involve incontinence or similar difficulties and will often be accompanied by psychological aggravation.

(b) Cases of sterility usually fall into one of two categories: surgical, chemical and disease cases (which involve no traumatic injury or scarring) and traumatic injuries (frequently caused by assaults) which are often aggravated by scarring.

The most serious cases merit awards approaching £55,000

The bottom of the range is the case of the much older man and merits an award of about £8,500

(c) An uncomplicated case of infertility without any aggravating features for a young man without children. £25,000 to £30,000

17

(d) A similar case but involving a family man who might have intended to have more children. £11,000 to £13,500

(e) Cases where the infertility amounts to little more than an 'insult'. £2,250

Female

(a) Infertility with associated depression and some anxiety and some pain and scarring. £48,000 to £65,000

(b) Infertility without any complication and where the Plaintiff already has children. £8,000 to £16,250

Where there are no complications and the Plaintiff already has children the award will be at the lower end of the bracket. The situation is, however, almost always complicated by significant psychological damage which will take it to the upper end of the bracket.

(c) Infertility where the Plaintiff would not have had children in any event (for example, because of age). £2,750 to £5,500

(d) Failed sterilisation leading to unwanted pregnancy. £8,000 to £11,000

(F) Kidney

(a) Serious and permanent damage to or loss of both kidneys. £65,000 to £80,000

(b) Where there is a significant risk of future urinary tract infection or other total loss of natural kidney function, the range is up to £27,000

Such cases will invariably carry with them substantial future medical expenses which, in this field, are particularly high.

(c) Loss of one kidney, with no damage to the other. £13,500 to £19,000

(G) Bowels

(a) Total loss of natural function and dependence on colostomy, depending on age. Up to £60,000

(b) Severe abdominal injury causing impairment of function and often necessitating temporary colostomy (leaving disfiguring scars) and/or restriction on employment and on diet. £20,000 to £30,000

(c) Penetrating injuries causing some permanent damage but an eventual return to natural function and control. £5,500 to £11,000

(H) Bladder

Awards for loss of bladder function have, surprisingly, often been higher than in bowel cases. This is probably because they often result from carcinogenic exposure (typically to antioxidants such as Nonox S in the rubber industry). The reported decisions are seriously out of date and the indexing-up procedure may be misleading.

(a) Complete loss of natural function and control. Up to £55,000

(b) Impairment of control with some pain and incontinence. £27,500 to £32,500

(c) Where there has been an almost complete recovery but some fairly long-term interference with natural function. £11,000 to £13,500

The cancer risk cases still occupy a special category and can properly attract awards at the top of the ranges even where natural function continues for the time being. However, these cases will now be more appropriately dealt with by provisional awards of a low level (£5,000) unless the foreseeable prognosis and outcome is clear. Once the prognosis is firm and reliable the award will reflect any loss of life expectancy, the level of continuing pain and suffering and most significantly the extent to which the Plaintiff has to live with the knowledge of the consequences which his death will have for others. The appropriate award for the middle-aged family man or woman whose life expectancy is reduced by 15 or 20 years is £20,000 to £30,000.

(I) Spleen

This is a very common injury, resulting, for example, from a very large number of motor cycle accidents: it is the classic handlebar injury.

(a) Loss of spleen where there is a continuing risk of internal infection and disorders due to the damage to the immune system. £5,500 to £8,750

(b) Where the above risks are not present or are minimal. £2,000 to £3,750

(J) Hernia

(a) Continuing pain and/or limitations on physical activities, sport or employment. £6,500 to £11,000

(b) Direct (where no pre-existing weakness) inguinal hernia, with some risk of recurrence. £3,000 to £4,000

(c) Uncomplicated indirect inguinal hernia with no other associated abdominal injury or damage. £1,500 to £2,750

6. Orthopaedic Injuries

(A) Neck Injuries

Neck injuries cover a very wide range. At one end of the spectrum is the injury which shatters a life and leaves the victim very severely disabled. This may have a value in excess of £60,000.

At the other end of the spectrum is the minor strain which causes the injured person to be off work for, say, three weeks and to suffer symptoms for, say, five weeks. This type of injury could attract an award of about £1,000.

The neck injury giving rise to symptoms for, say, a couple of weeks would attract no more than about £500.

(a) Neck injury associated with incomplete paraplegia or resulting in permanent spastic quadriparesis or where, despite the wearing of a collar 24 hours a day for a period of years, the neck could still not move and severe headaches have proved intractable. £60,000

(b) Injury falling short of the disability in (a) but being of considerable severity; e.g., permanent damage to the brachial plexus £27,500 to £50,000

(c) The injury is such as to cause severe damage to soft tissues and/or ruptured tendons and

results in significant disability of a permanent
nature. In the region of £22,500

The precise award depends on the length of
any recovery period and the prognosis.

(d) Injuries such as fractures or dislocation
causing severe immediate symptoms or
necessitating spinal fusion leaving significantly impaired function or vulnerability
to further trauma, pain and limitation of
activities. £11,000 to £14,500

(e) Whiplash or wrenching-type injury and disc
lesion of the more severe type, if they result in
cervical spondylosis, serious limitation of
movement, permanent or recurring pain, stiffness or discomfort, the potential need for
further surgery or increased vulnerability to
trauma. £6,000 to £11,000

(f) Relatively minor injuries which may or may
not have exacerbated or accelerated some
pre-existing unrelated condition but with, in
any event, a complete recovery within a few
years. This bracket will also apply to moderate
whiplash injuries where the period of recovery
is fairly protracted and where there is an
increased vulnerability to further trauma. £3,250 to £6,000

(g) Minor soft tissue and whiplash injuries and the
like where symptoms are moderate and full
recovery takes place within, at most, two
years. Up to £3,250

(B) Back Injuries

Subject to injuries involving paralysis (e.g. quadriplegia) which are dealt with elsewhere, relatively
few back injuries command awards above £20,000.
Those that do, depend upon special features.

(a) The most severe of back injuries which fall short of paralysis but the results of which include, for example, impotence.   £43,000 to £65,000

(b) Special features exist which take the particular injury outside any lower bracket applicable to orthopaedic damage to the back; e.g. impaired bladder and bowel function, severe sexual difficulties and unsightly scarring. In the region of   £35,000

(c) Serious back injury, involving disc lesions or fractures of discs or vertebral bodies where, despite treatment, there remains continuing pain and discomfort, impaired agility and sexual function, depression, personality change, alcoholism, unemployability and the risk of arthritis.   £17,500 to £28,000

(d) Permanent residual disability albeit of less severity than in the higher bracket.   £12,500 to £17,500

This bracket contains a large number of different types of injury; e.g. a crush fracture of the lumbar vertebrae with 40% risk of osteoarthritis and constant pain and discomfort and impaired sexual function, or traumatic spondylolisthesis with continuous pain and 70% likelihood of spinal fusion, or prolapsed intervertebral disc with substantial acceleration of back degeneration.

(e) Moderate Back Injuries   £5,500 to £12,500

A wide variety of injuries qualify for inclusion within this bracket. The precise figure depends upon the severity of the original injury and/or the existence of some permanent or chronic disability.

Examples are

(i)   the disturbance of ligaments and muscles causing backache

23

(ii)   soft tissue injuries resulting in exacerbation of a back condition and

(iii) a prolapsed disc necessitating a laminectomy or resulting in repeated relapses.

(f)   Minor Back Injuries   Up to £5,500

For example, strains, sprains and disc prolapses and soft tissue injuries which have made a full recovery or resulted only in minor continuing disability or which have accelerated or exacerbated pre-existing unrelated conditions for a fairly brief period of time.

(C) Injuries to the Pelvis and Hips

At its worst the most serious hip and pelvic injury can be as devastating as a leg amputation and accordingly will attract a similar award of damages. The upper limit generally will be in the region of £30,000. Where, however, there are specific sequelae of exceptional severity the case would be one calling for a higher award.

(a) Extensive fractures of the pelvis involving, for example, dislocation of a low back joint and a ruptured bladder or a hip injury resulting in spondylolisthesis of a low back joint with intolerable pain necessitating spinal fusion. Substantial residual disabilities, such as a complicated arthrodesis with residual lack of bowel and bladder control, sexual dysfunction or hip deformity necessitating the use of a caliper, will be inevitable.   £32,500 to £50,000

(b) Injuries only a little less serious but with particular distinguishing features taking them out of any lower bracket.   £27,500 to £32,500

Examples are a fracture dislocation of the pelvis involving both ischial and pubic rami, resulting in impotence or traumatic myositis ossificans with formation of ectopic bone around the hip.

(c)	**Serious Injury to the Hip or Pelvis**	£17,500 to £22,500

A variety of injuries fall within this bracket, such as a fracture of the acetabulum leading to degenerative changes and leg instability requiring an osteotomy and the likelihood of hip relacement surgery in the years ahead; or the fracture of an arthritic femur or hip necessitating the insertion of a hip joint; or a fracture resulting in hip replacement surgery being only partially successful with a clear risk of the need for revision surgery.

(d) Significant injury to the pelvis or hip but where any permanent disability is not major and any future risk is not great. £12,000 to £17,500

(e) **Injuries of Limited Severity** £5,750 to £12,000

In cases where hip replacement has been carried out wholly successfully the award would fall towards the top of the bracket. The bracket will also include cases where hip replacement is anticipated.

(f) Relatively minor hip or pelvic injuries with no residual disability. Up to £5,750

(D) Amputation of Arms

(a) **Loss of Both Arms** £90,000 to £105,000

There is no recent case to offer guidance but the effect of such an injury is to reduce a person with full awareness to a state of considerable helplessness.

25

(b) Loss of One Arm

The value of a lost arm depends upon:

(i)   Whether it is amputated below or above the elbow. The loss of the additional joint obviously adds greatly to the disability.

(ii)   Whether or not the amputation was of the dominant arm.

(iii)   The intensity of any phantom pains.

(1)	*Arm amputated at the shoulder*	Not less than £57,500
(2)	*Above elbow amputation*	£46,000 to £50,000

A shorter stump may create difficulties in the successful use of a prosthesis. This will make the level of the award towards the top end of the bracket. Amputation through the elbow however will normally produce an award at the bottom end of the bracket.

(3)	*Below elbow amputation*	£40,000 to £46,000

Amputation through the forearm with residual severe organic and phantom pains would attract an award at the top end of the bracket.

(E) Other Arm Injuries

(a) Severe Injuries   £40,000 to £50,000

Injuries which in terms of their severity fall short of amputation but which are extremely serious in their own right and leave the Plaintiff little better off than if he had lost his arm.

(b) **Injuries Resulting in Permanent and Substantial Disablement** £17,500 to £24,000

Examples are serious fractures of one or both forearms where there is significant permanent residual disability whether functional or cosmetic.

(c) **Less Severe Injury** £8,500 to £17,500

While there will have been significant disabilities, a substantial degree of recovery will have taken place or will be anticipated.

(d) **Simple Fractures of the Forearm** £2,750 to £8,500

Uncomplicated fractures of the radius and/or ulna with a complete recovery within a short time would justify an award of £2,750. Injuries resulting in modest residual disability or deformity would merit an award toward the upper end of this bracket.

(F) Shoulder Injuries

Unless associated with a severe neck, back or arm injury, shoulder injuries tend to attract modest awards of well under five figures.

(a) **Serious Injury** £5,750 to £8,500

Dislocation of the shoulder and damage to the lower part of the brachial plexus causing pain in shoulder and neck, aching in elbow, sensory symptoms with forearm and hand and weakness of grip.

(b) **Moderate Injury** £3,500 to £5,500

Frozen shoulder with limitation of movement and discomfort with symptoms persisting for between one and two years.

(c) Minor Injury   £2,000 to £3,500

Soft tissue injury to shoulder with considerable pain but almost complete recovery in less
than one year.

(d) Fracture of Clavicle

The level of the award will depend on whether
union is anatomically displaced.   £1,500 to £3,000

(G) Injuries to the Elbow

(a) A Severely Disabling Injury   £17,250 to £23,000

(b) Less Severe Injuries   £8,000 to £14,000

These injuries lead to impairment of function
but do not involve major surgery or significant
disability.

(c) Moderate or Minor Injury   Up to £5,500

Most elbow injuries fall into this category.
They comprise a simple fracture, tennis elbow
syndrome and lacerations; i.e. those injuries
which cause no permanent damage and do not
result in any permanent impairment of function.

(H) Wrist Injuries

(a) Injuries resulting in complete loss of function
in the wrist.   £21,500 to £24,000

(b) Injury resulting in significant permanent
residual disability.   £11,000 to £17,250

(c) Less severe but still permanent disability as,
for example, persisting pain and stiffness.   £5,500 to £11,000

(d) Where recovery is complete the award will rarely exceed   £4,500

(e) An uncomplicated Colles' fracture.   £3,250

(I) Hand Injuries

Of the arm, the hand is both functionally and cosmetically the most important feature. The loss of a hand is valued not far short of the amount which would be awarded for loss of an arm. The upper end of any bracket will generally be appropriate where the material injury is to the dominant hand.

(a) Total Effective Loss of Both Hands   £55,000 to £75,000

Serious injury resulting in extensive damage to both hands such as to render them little more than useless will justify an award of £55,000. The top of the bracket is applicable where no effective prosthesis can be used.

(b) Serious damage to both hands giving rise to permanent cosmetic disability and significant loss of function.   £24,000 to £35,000

(c) Total or Effective Loss of One Hand   £40,000 to £46,000

This bracket will apply to a hand which was crushed and thereafter surgically amputated or where all fingers and most of the palm have been traumatically amputated. The upper end of the bracket is indicated where the hand so damaged was the dominant one.

(d) Amputation of index, middle and/or ring fingers, rendering hand of very little use with exceedingly weak grip.   £27,000 to £38,000

(e) Serious Hand Injuries   Up to £27,000

For example, loss reducing hand to 50% capacity with, e.g. several fingers amputated and rejoined to hand leaving it clawed, clumsy and unsightly or amputation of some fingers together with part of the palm resulting in gross diminution of grip and dexterity and gross cosmetic disfigurement.

(f) Severe fractures to fingers with partial amputations and resulting in deformity, impairment of grip, reduced mechanical function and disturbed sensation.   Up to £16,250

(g) Maximum for Total Loss of Index Finger   £8,500

(h) Partial loss of index finger or injury giving rise to disfigurement and impairment of grip or dexterity.   £5,500 to £8,000

(i) Fracture of Index Finger   £4,000 to £5,500

This level is appropriate where a fracture has mended quickly but grip has remained impaired, there is pain on heavy use and osteoarthritis is likely in due course.

(j) Total Loss of Middle Finger   £7,000

(k) Serious Injury to Ring or Middle Fingers   £6,500 to £7,250

The top of this bracket is the maximum figure for serious injury involving either of these fingers. Fractures causing stiffness, deformity and permanent loss of grip or dexterity will also fall within this bracket.

(l) Loss of terminal phalanx of the ring or middle fingers.   £2,000 to £3,250

(m) Amputation of little finger   £3,750 to £5,500

(n) Loss of part of the little finger where the remaining tip is sensitive.   £2,000 to £2,500

(o) Amputation of Ring and Little Fingers   £9,750

(p) Amputation of the terminal phalanges of the index and middle fingers with further injury to the fourth finger, scarring and restriction of movement with grip and fine handling impaired.   £11,000

(q) Fracture of one finger with complete recovery within a few weeks.   £1,000 to £1,600

(r) **Loss of Thumb**   £16,000 to £24,500

(s) **Very Serious Injury to Thumb**   £9,000 to £14,250

This bracket is appropriate where the thumb has been severed at the base and grafted back on leaving a virtually useless and grossly deformed digit or where the thumb has been amputated through the metacarpo-phalangeal joint.

(t) Injury to thumb involving amputation of tip, nerve damage or fracture necessitating insertion of wires, and operative treatment leaving thumb cold and ultra-sensitive, or leading to impairment of grip and loss of manual dexterity   £5,750 to £7,500

(u) **Moderate Injuries to the Thumb**   £4,250 to £5,750

Such as injuries necessitating arthrodesis of the interphalangeal joint or causing damage to tendons or nerves and in either event resulting in impairment of sensation and function and cosmetic deformity.

(v) **Severe Dislocation of the Thumb**   £2,000 to £2,750

(w) **Minor Injuries to the Thumb**   £2,000

For example, a fracture which has recovered in six months except for residual stiffness and discomfort.

31

(x) Trivial thumb injuries such as cause severe pain for a very short time and which have cleared up within a very few months. £900

(y) **Cases of Vibration White Finger**

This is a particular form of Raynaud's phenomenon caused by prolonged exposure to vibration.

(i) Extensive blanching of most fingers with episodes in summer and winter of such severity as to necessitate changing occupation to avoid further exposure to vibration. £4,000 to £6,000

(ii) Blanching of one or more fingers with numbness. Usually occurring only in winter and causing slight interference with home and social activities. £2,000

(iii) Blanching of one or more fingertips, with or without tingling and numbness. £900

(J) Work-related Upper Limb Disorders

This section covers a range of upper limb injury in the form of the following pathological conditions from finger to elbow.

(a) Tenosynovitis. Inflammation of synovial sheaths of tendons usually resolving with rest over a short period. Sometimes it leads to continuing symptoms of loss of grip and dexterity.

(b) De Quervain's tenosynovitis. A form of tenosynovitis, rarely bilateral, involving inflammation of the tendons of the thumb.

(c) Tenovaginitis stenovans. Otherwise trigger finger/thumb: thickening of tendons.

(d) Carpal tunnel syndrome. Constriction of the median nerve of the wrist or thickening of surrounding tissue, often relieved by decompression operation.

(e) Epicondylitis. Inflammation in the elbow joint: medial (golfer's elbow), lateral (tennis elbow).

The various levels of award below apply to each such condition. The following considerations affect the level of award regardless of the precise condition:

(i)   Bilateral or one-sided

(ii)   Level of symptoms (pain, swelling, tenderness, crepitus)

(iii) Ability to work

(iv)   Capacity to avoid recurrence of symptoms

(a) Continuing bilateral disability with surgery and loss of employment   £9,750 to £10,250

(b) Continuing symptoms, but fluctuating and unilateral   £6,500 to £7,000

(c) Symptoms resolving over two years   £3,750 to £4,250

(d) Complete recovery within a short period   £1,000 to £1,350

(K) Leg Injuries

Leg injuries span the entire spectrum of quantum assessment brackets from the lower hundreds of pounds for, e.g. severe bruising, to six-figure awards for injuries of the utmost severity.

It is probably helpful to think of leg injuries in terms of:

    (i)   Amputations, which frequently result in severe 'phantom pain' in addition to loss of function (£37,500 to £105,000)

    (ii)   Severe leg injuries (£13,500 to £60,000)

    (iii) Other leg injuries (£12,500 or less)

(a) Total Loss of Both Legs   £95,000 to £105,000

This is the appropriate award where both legs are lost above the knee and particularly if near to the hip leaving a stump less than adequate to accommodate a useful prosthesis.

(b) Below Knee Amputations of Both Legs   £80,000 to £100,000

The top of the bracket is appropriate where both legs are amputated just below the knee. Amputations further down result in a lower award.

(c) Above Knee Amputation of One Leg   £40,000 to £54,000

The area within the bracket in which the award should fall will depend upon such factors as the height of the amputation, the severity of phantom pains, whether or not there have been any problems with a prosthesis, any side effects, such as backache or depression.

(d) Below Knee Amputation of One Leg   £37,500 to £50,000

The straightforward case of a below knee amputation with no complications would justify an award at the bottom of this bracket. At or towards the top of the range would come the traumatic amputation in a horrendous accident, where the injured person remained fully conscious or where attempts to save the leg resulted in numerous operations with surgical amputation taking place years after the event.

(e) Leg Injuries

(i) There are some injuries which, although not involving amputation of the leg, are nevertheless so severe that the courts have awarded damages in the same region. Examples would be a degloving injury from knee to ankle, gross shortening of the leg, non-union of fractures and extensive bone grafting. £40,000 to £54,000

(ii) Awards within this bracket will be made where the injuries leave permanent disability necessitating the use of crutches for the remainder of a person's life and very limited walking capacity; where multiple fractures have taken years to heal with resulting leg deformity and limitation of movement; or where arthrosis has developed in e.g. the knee joint and further surgical treatment is likely to be necessary. £24,000 to £35,000

(iii) A claim may be brought within this bracket by reason of such factors as significant damage to a joint or ligaments causing instability, prolonged treatment or a lengthy period non-weight bearing, substantial and unsightly scarring, the likelihood of arthrodesis to the hip, the near certainty of arthritis setting in, the gross restriction of walking capacity and the need for hip replacement. A combination of such features will be necessary to justify such an award. £17,250 to £24,000

(iv) This level of award still applies to relatively serious injuries, including severe, complicated or multiple fractures. The position of an award within this bracket will be influenced by the

35

period of time off work and by the presence or risk of degenerative changes, imperfect union of fractures, muscle wasting, limited joint movements, instability of the knee, unsightly scarring and permanently increased vulnerability to damage.   £12,500 to £17,250

(v)   Most awards that fall within this range comprise fractures where there has been incomplete recovery. Examples are:

A defective gait, a limp, impaired mobility, sensory loss, discomfort or an exacerbation of a pre-existing disability.   £8,000 to £12,500

(vi)   Simple fracture of femur, with no damage to articular surfaces   Up to £6,500

(vii)   A simple fracture of the tibia or fibula with complete recovery will attract a figure towards the top of the bracket. Below that level will be a variety of different types of soft tissue injuries, lacerations, cuts, severe bruising or contusions all of which will have recovered completely or almost completely, with any residual disability comprising scarring or being of a minor nature.   Up to £4,000

(L) Knee Injuries

Knee injuries fall within a bracket extending from a few hundred pounds for a simple twisting injury up to £40,000 or so where there have been considerable problems leading to an arthrodesis.

(a)   This bracket is appropriate to the serious knee injury where there has been disruption of the joints, gross ligamentous damage, lengthy treatment, considerable pain and loss of

function and an arthrodesis has taken place or
is inevitable.   £30,000 to £40,000

(b) This applies where a leg fracture extends into
the knee-joint causing pain which is constant,
permanent, limits movement or impairs agility and renders the injured person prone to
osteoarthritis and the risk of arthrodesis.   £22,500 to £30,000

(c) The injuries justifying awards falling within
this bracket are less serious than those in the
higher bracket and/or result in less severe
disability. There may be continuing symptoms
by way of pain or discomfort and limitation of
movement or instability and deformity with
the risk of degenerative changes occurring in
the long term, consequent upon ligamentous
or meniscal injury, damage to the kneecap or
muscular wasting.   £12,000 to £19,000

(d) This bracket is appropriate to cases involving
a torn cartilage or meniscus, dislocation,
ligamentous damage and the like or injuries
which accelerate symptoms from a pre-existing condition but which injuries additionally
result in minor instability, wasting, weakness
or other mild future disability.   £6,500 to £12,000

(e) Awards in this bracket will be made in respect
of injuries less serious than but similar to
bracket (d) or in respect of lacerations, twisting or bruising injuries. Where recovery has
been complete the award is unlikely to exceed
£2,750. Injuries resulting in continuous aching
or discomfort or occasional pain will attract
awards towards the upper end of the bracket.   Up to £6,000

(M) Ankle Injuries

The vast majority of ankle injuries are worth
significantly less than £10,000. The ceiling, however, is about £30,000 where the degree of disablement is very severe.

(a) Examples of injuries which would attract awards in this bracket are limited and unusual. They would include the following:

Transmalleolar fracture of the ankle with extensive soft tissue damage resulting in deformity and the risk that any future injury to the leg might necessitate a below knee amputation. Bilateral ankle fractures causing degeneration of the joints at a young age necessitating arthrodesis.

£22,000 to £30,000

(b) Awards in this bracket are justified where the ankle injury is severe necessitating an extensive period of treatment and/or a lengthy period in plaster or with pins and plates inserted and where there is significant residual disability by way of ankle instability, severely limited ability to walk etc. The position within the bracket will, in part, be determined by, e.g. a failed arthrodesis, regular disturbance of sleep, unsightly operational scarring and any need to wear special footwear.

£14,250 to £22,000

(c) In this area fall the fractures, ligamentous tears and the like, giving rise to less serious disabilities such as difficulty walking over uneven ground, awkwardness on stairs, irritation from metal plates and residual scarring.

£6,000 to £12,000

(d) Awards at and below £6,000 are appropriate for less serious, minor or undisplaced fractures, sprains and ligamentous injuries. The position within the scale would be determined by whether or not a complete recovery has been made and if not whether there is any tendency for the ankle to give way, any scarring, aching or discomfort, or the possibility of later osteoarthritis.

Up to £6,000

(N) Achilles Tendon

(a) Where there has been severance of the tendon and peroneus longus muscle giving rise to cramp, swelling and restricted ankle movement necessitating the cessation of active sports. £16,250 to £17,750

(b) This figure is appropriate for an injury resulting in complete division of the tendon, followed by a successful repair operation but leaving residual weakness, a limitation of ankle movements, a limp and residual scarring with further improvement unlikely. £11,000 to £13,500

(c) Complete division of the tendon but with no significant functional disability. £6,500 to £8,000

(d) Ankle turned resulting in damage to tendon and feeling of being unsure of ankle support. £3,250 to £4,250

(O) Foot Injuries

(a) Amputation of Both Feet £65,000 to £70,000

(b) Amputation of One Foot £35,000 to £46,000

These injuries justify an award similar to that applicable to the below knee amputation of both legs or one leg. The loss of a useful ankle joint is common to both kinds of amputation.

(c) Few foot injuries fall within this bracket. In order to do so there would have to be permanent and severe pain or really serious disability. Such injuries would include traumatic amputation of the forefoot when its effect was to exacerbate a pre-existing back problem and where there was a significant risk of the need for complete amputation. Similarly an injury resulting in the loss of a substantial portion of the heel and limited mobility.

£35,000 to £46,000

(d) This level of award is suitable for severe injuries, such as where there have been fractures to both heels or feet with substantially restricted mobility or considerable or permanent pain in both feet. This bracket is also suitable to unusually severe injuries to a single foot which have resulted in heel fusion, osteoporosis, ulceration or other disability preventing the wearing of ordinary shoes.

£20,000 to £28,500

(e) Towards the top end of this bracket would come the injury resulting in grievous burns to both feet requiring several operations but nevertheless leaving disfiguring scars and persisting irritation.

Lower in the bracket are those injuries which are less severe but nevertheless result in fusion of foot joints, continuing pain from traumatic arthritis, prolonged treatment and the future risk of osteoarthritis.

£11,250 to £17,500

(f) This bracket is appropriate for displaced metatarsal fractures resulting in permanent deformity and continuing symptoms.

£6,000 to £11,250

(g) This level of award applies to the relatively modest injuries such as metatarsal fractures, ruptured ligaments, puncture wounds and the like. Continuing symptoms, such as a permanent limp, pain or aching would justify an award between £3,000 and £6,000. Straightforward foot injuries by way of fractures, lacerations, contusions etc. resulting in complete or near complete recoveries would justify awards of £3,000 or less.

Up to £6,000

(P) Toe Injuries

(a) Amputation of all Toes   £16,250 to £24,250

The position in the bracket will be determined
by, for example, whether or not the amputation was traumatic or surgical, and the extent
of loss of the forefoot, and residual effects on
mobility.

(b) Amputation of Great Toe, in the region of   £13,500

(c) This is the appropriate bracket for severe crush
injuries, falling short of the need for amputation or necessitating only partial amputation.
It also includes bursting wounds and injuries
resulting in severe damage and in any event
producing continuing significant symptoms.   £11,000 to £13,500

(d) This bracket will apply to serious fractures of
the great toe or to crush and multiple fractures
of any toes. There would have to be some
permanent disability by way of discomfort,
pain or sensitive scarring to justify an award
within this bracket. A number of unsuccessful
operations, stabbing pain, impaired gait and
the like would place the award towards the top
end of the bracket.   £6,000 to £8,500

(e) This level of award applies to modest injuries
including relatively straightforward fractures
or the exacerbation of a pre-existing degenerative condition.

Only £2,750 or less would be awarded for
straightforward fractures of one or more toes
with complete resolution within a short period
of time down to the minor injuries involving
lacerations, cuts, contusions and bruises, all of
which would have had a complete or near
complete recovery.   Up to £4,000

41

7. Facial Injuries

The assessment of general damages for facial injuries is an extremely difficult task, there being two elements which complicate the award.

First, while in most of the cases dealt with below the injuries described are skeletal, many of them will involve an element of disfigurement or at least cosmetic disability.

Secondly, in cases where there is a cosmetic element the courts have invariably drawn a distinction between the awards of damages to males and females, the latter attracting the higher awards.

The subject of burns is not dealt with separately because burns of any degree of severity tend to be so devastating as to be invariably at the upper ends of the brackets.

In the guidance which follows some effort has been made to distinguish these types of cases but the above considerations must always be borne in mind. Where there is a cosmetic element care must be taken to endeavour to remain broadly within the guidelines which are extracted from reported decisions wherein a subjective element was taken into account.

(A) Skeletal Injuries

(a) Le Fort fractures of frontal facial bones. £11,000 to £16,000

(b) Multiple fractures of facial bones involving some facial deformity of a permanent nature. £6,750 to £11,000

(c) Fracture of Nose

(i) Simple undisplaced with full recovery £875

(ii) Displaced fracture requiring no more than manipulation £1,100 to £1,350

(iii) Displaced where recovery complete but only after surgery £1,750 to £2,000

(iv) Serious fractures requiring a number of operations and resulting in permanent damage to airways and/or facial deformity. £4,750 to £8,000

(d) Fractures of Cheekbones

(i) Simple fracture of cheekbones for which no surgery is required and a complete recovery is effected. £1,100 to £1,350

(ii) Simple fracture of cheekbones for which some reconstructive surgery is necessary but from which there is a complete recovery with no or only minimal cosmetic effects. £2,000 to £2,750

(iii) Serious fractures requiring surgery but with lasting consequences such as paraesthesia in the cheeks or the lips or some element of disfigurement. £4,500 to £7,000

(e) Fractures of Jaws

(i) Simple fracture requiring immobilisation but from which recovery is complete. £2,750 to £3,750

43

(ii)	Serious fracture with permanent consequences such as difficulty in opening the mouth or with eating or where there is paraesthesia in the area of the jaw.	£8,000 to £13,500
(iii)	Very serious fractures followed by prolonged treatment and permanent consequences, including severe pain, restriction in eating, paraesthesia and/or the risk of arthritis in the joints.	£13,500 to £20,000

(f) Damage to Teeth

In these cases there will generally have been a course of dental treatment. The amounts awarded will vary as to the extent and discomfort of such treatment. Costs incurred to the date of trial will, of course, be special damage but it will often be necessary to award a capital sum in respect of the cost of future dental treatment.

(i)	Loss of One Front Tooth	£1,000 to £1,600
(ii)	Loss of Two Front Teeth	£2,000 to £2,500
(iii)	Loss of or Serious Damage to Several Front Teeth	£3,750 to £4,750
(iv)	Loss of or Damage to Back Teeth: per Tooth	£500 to £800

(B) Facial Disfigurement

In this class of case the distinction between male and female and the subjective approach are of particular significance.

(a) Females

(i)	Very severe facial scarring in a relatively young girl (teens to early thirties) where the cosmetic effect is very disfiguring and the psychological reaction severe.	£22,000 to £40,000

(ii)   Less severe scarring where the disfigurement is still substantial and where there is a significant psychological reaction.   £13,500 to £22,000

(iii)   Significant scarring where the worst effects have been or will be reduced by plastic surgery leaving some cosmetic disability and where the psychological reaction is not great or having been considerable at the outset has diminished to relatively minor proportions.   £8,000 to £13,500

(iv)   Some scarring but not of great significance, either because there is but one scar which can be camouflaged or because although there are a large number of very small scars the overall effect is to mar but not markedly to affect the appearance and where the reaction is no more than that of an ordinarily sensitive young woman.   £1,500 to £6,000

(b) Males

(i)   Particularly severe facial scars especially in males under 30, where there is permanent disfigurement even after plastic surgery and a considerable element of psychological reaction.   £13,500 to £27,500

(ii)   Severe facial scarring leaving moderate to severe permanent disfigurement.   £8,000 to £13,500

(iii)   Significant but not severe scars which will remain visible at conversational distances.   £4,000 to £8,000

(iv)   Relatively minor scarring which is not particularly prominent except on close inspection.   £1,500 to £4,000

(v)   Trivial scarring where the effect is minor only.   £800 to £1,500

8. Scarring to Other Parts of the Body

This is an area in which it is not possible to offer much useful guidance. The principles are the same as those applied to cases of facial disfigurement and the brackets are broadly the same. It must be remembered that many of the physical injuries already described involve some element of disfigurement and that element is of course taken into account in suggesting the appropriate bracket. There of course remain some cases where the element of disfigurement is the predominant one in the assessment of damages. Where the scarring is not to the face or is not usually visible then the awards will tend to be lower than those for facial or readily visible disfigurement.

The effects of burns will normally be regarded as more serious since they tend to cause a greater degree of pain and to lead to greater disfigurement.

There is, however, one area in which an almost 'conventional' figure has emerged. In cases where an exploratory laparotomy has been performed but no significant internal injury has been found the award for the operation and the inevitable scar is of the order of £3,500.

9. Damage to Hair

(a) Damage to hair in consequence of permanent waving, tinting or the like, where the effects are tingling or 'burning' of the scalp causing dry, brittle hair, which breaks off and/or falls out leading to distress, depression, embarrassment and loss of confidence, and inhibiting social life. In the more serious cases thinning continues and the prospects of regrowth are poor or there has been total loss of areas of hair and regrowth is slow.   £3,000 to £5,000

(b) Less serious versions of the above where symptoms are fewer or only of a minor character; also, cases where hair has been pulled out leaving bald patches. The level of the award will depend on the length of time taken before regrowth occurs.   £1,750 to £3,000

Index